Darkness Into Light

Darkness Into Light

John Robinson

authorHOUSE®

AuthorHouse™ UK Ltd.
1663 Liberty Drive
Bloomington, IN 47403 USA
www.authorhouse.co.uk
Phone: 0800.197.4150

Published by AuthorHouse   02/25/2014

ISBN: 978-1-4918-9674-7 (sc)
ISBN: 978-1-4918-9675-4 (e)

Contents

BOOK 2

This Book is dedicated to
my Mother Ellen.

My friend.

Introduction

This Book is for people looking for:

* Trying to find inner peace
* Trying to get in touch with your inner self
* Looking to for a Pathway out of Depression

Depression will go away one day!
It's important to cling onto that fact.

A WORD

A careless word may kindle strife

A cruel word
May wreck a life

A bitter word
May hate in still

A brutal word
May smite and kill

A gracious word
May light a day

A timely word
May lessen stress

A loving word
May heal and bless

Happiness

Happiness does not so much consist
In having much to enjoy, as in the
Faculty to enjoy life.

He who cannot be happy without
Taking great pains
Will always find the pains
Greater than his happiness.

Worry

Worry is the result of not minding
Our own business,
and generally means thinking of
something in the future.
The next step is clear
The step after is not my look out,
But gods

A Song of Hope

From the deepest night and longest
rise's morn
Out of the long and weary waiting
Hope is born
Therefore let us wait the breaking
Of the dawn.

Priceless gems in earths dark places
Often are found
And the lovely violets nestle
Near the ground
So mid toil and hard endeavour
Work is crowned

Who shall praise the night consolations
Bright hope brings
Who shall land enough the lustre
Of the her wings
Only those who pause and listen
When she sings

Those who are constrained to solicit
For assistance are really to be pitied
Those who receive it without are to
Be envied; but those who bestow it
Unasked are to be admired.

Never stoop to do or say anything
That is beneath the dignity of the
Character to which you aspire.

Loving act

A loving act does more good than
A fiery exhortation
What mankind needs is not more
Good talkers but more good Samaritans.

One day

An element of weakness is much of our
resolving, is that we try to grasp too much
of life at one time.
We think of it as a whole, instead
Of taking the days one by one.
Life is a sunrise and each tiny piece must
be cut and set with skill.

If

If we knew the cares and trials
Knew the efforts, all in vain
And the bitter disappointment
Understood the loss and gain
Would the grim eternal roughness
Seem, I wonder, just the same?
Should we help where now we hinder?

Should we pity where we blame?
Could we judge all deeds by motives
That surround each other lives
See the naked heart and spirit,
Know what spice the action gives;
Often we could find it better

Just to judge all action good,
We should love each other better,
If we only understood

Peace

It is done:
Clang of bells, roar of gun,
Send the tidings up and down;

How the belfries rock and real,
How the great guns peal on peal,
Fling the joy from town to town.

Selfish

Oh! If the selfish knew how much
they host,
What would they not endeavour,
not endure,
To imitate as far as in them lay
Him, who this wisdom and his
power employs
In making others happy?

To Plan

I would not dare, though it were
offered me

To plan my lot far but a single day,

So sure am I that all my life would be

Marked with a blot in token of my sway.

Did you ever try the gospel of smiles?
A smile is a sunbeam of the soul.
It lights up the eye and transfigures
the countenance.
A frown is easier but gives no light.
Open the soul windows and let in the
light, and keep these windows open;
Then let out light in smiles.
A smile can scatter gloom and
silver-line a cloud.
It costs little, but counts for much.
Tears and smiles lie near together.
Dry your tears and scatter your smiles.

To Love

It is the nature of genuine love never
to tire.
If you are tired of loving,
You have never loved.

One day at a time

One day at a time, a burden to great
To be born for two can be born for one;
Who knows what will enter-to-
morrows gate;
While yet we are speaking all may
be done.

One day at a time—but a single day,
Whatever its load, whatever its length;
And there's a bit precious scripture to say
That according to each shall be
our strength.

Hope and Faith

Hope is the scented flower
Which in the heart implanted,
When words have swept bosom's power,
Still blossoms like a thing enchanted,
Life sweet inheritance and dower.

Faith is the steady spark,
For journeying mortals lighted,
Still beaming star like through the dark
On high, where rest by sorrow sighted,
And still where lifted eyes my mark.

The Mothers of Men

The bravest battle that ever was fought
Shall I tell you when and where?
On the maps of the world you will find
it not,
Tis fought by mothers of men.
But deep in a wall'd up woman's heart
Of women that would not yield,
Bur bravely, silently bore her part,
Lo, there is the battlefield.

<u>Morning</u>

O word and thing most beautiful!
Our yesterday was hard and dull,
Gray mists obscured its noonday sun,
Its evening sobbed and wept rain
But to and fro in hiding night
Some healing angel swift has run
And all is fresh and fair again.

O word and thing most beautiful!
The hearts that were of cares so full,
The tired hands, the tired feet,
So glad of night, are glad of morn!
Where are the clouds of yesterday?
The world is good, the world is sweet,
And life is new, and hope reborn!

Smile

Keep a task in your hand: you
must labour,
By toil is true happiness won,
For foe, and for friend, and for neighbour,
Rejoice, there is much to be done
Endeavour by crowning life's duty
With joy-giving song and with smile,
To make the world fuller of beauty,
because you are in it a while.

Little Time

Since it is only such a little while
That we can be together, why fret at
The imperfections and blundering
Steps of those who walk by our side?
It is such a little way before the paths
Diverge, and they or we pass
Into the shadows,—why not take care
That only pleasant memories remain?

To Judge

How shall we judge their present,
We who have never seen
That which is past for ever and that
Which might have been?
Measuring by ourselves unwise
Indeed are we!
Measuring what we know by what
We can hardly see.

<u>Kindness</u>

Kindness is a language which the
Dumb can speak and the deaf
can understand.

Power

The power to love truly and devotedly
Is the noblest gift with which a human
being can be endowed.

<u>Right</u>

Consider well; weigh strictly right
and wrong.
Resolve quick; but resolved be strong
If to thyself thou canst thyself acquit,
Rather stand up alone than in
with millions.

Who is brave man? Who?
He who dares to defend the right
When right is miscalled wrong . . .
Who dares to do right whate'er betide
who, fearing god fears none beside—
This man hath courage true.

Love

Love without obedience is but
dis-simulation; and obedience without
love, but drudgery and slavery

Blessed be he who gives to the poor
Albeit only a penny; doubly blessed
Be he who adds kind words to his gift.
Say not, because thou canst not do
everything,
"I will do nothing"

<u>Tis</u>

'Tis well in deeds of good, though small
to thrive;
'Tis well some past of ill, though small
to cure
'Tis well with onward, upward hope
to strive;
'Tis better and diviner to endure

Let me not hide my talents;
Help me to use each precious gift
Thou givest as thou shalt choose.
Let me not self-love assail me,
Hiding thy face;
Let not my courage fail me,
Bur give thy grace.

John Robinson

Fix up

There are only two things in the world to
worry over,—the things you can
Control, and the things you can't control,
fix up the first to your liking, and forget
the second.

Three words

God bless thee! 'Tis the fondest wish.
A loving heart can hold;
What words of deepest tenderness
Those three words enfold

Brighter

Would you have the world better
or brighter?
Then light up the way you go;
Make some little part of it lighter with
beams from your life's steady glow.
Make the world you live in your debtor,
as through it you journey along;
Be good and the earth will grow better;
Do right, and the right will grow strong.

Our Neighbours

Somebody near you is struggling alone
Over life's desert sand;
Faith, hope, and courage together
are gone,
Reach him a helping hand.
Turn on his darkness a beam of
your light.
Kindle to guide him a beacon fire bright;
Cheer his discouragement, sooth
his affright,
Lovingly help him stand.
Somebody near you is hungry and cold
Send him some aid to-day;
Somebody near you is feeble and old,
Let without human aid
Under his burden put hands kind
and strong.
Speak to him tenderly,—sing him a song;
Haste to do something to help him along
Over his weary way

<u>On Entering Life</u>

Thy lifetime now dawning,
So new and so strange,
May bring to thee sorrow,
It will bring thee change.
But fear not, and doubt not,
For god is thy friend,
And he will be with thee
To guide and defend.

Home

The world with many paths is lined,
But one alone for me;
One little road where I may find
The charms I want to see.
Though thoroughfares majestic call
The multitude to roam,
I would not leave to know them all
The path that leads to home.

At The End

At the end of life we shall not be
Asked how much service we gave in it
Not how full of sacrifice;
Not how happy we were,
But how helpful we were;
Not how ambition was gratified,
But how love was served.

<u>See</u>

See the silent shadow moving
Life and time are worth improving;
Seize the moments whilst they stay,
Seize and use them lest thou lose them
And lament a wasted day

Risks

To laugh is risk appearing the fool
To weep is risk to appearing weak
To reach out is to risk involvement
To expose feelings is to risk exposing
your true self
To place ideas, your dreams before a
crowd is to risk their loss
To love is to risk not been loved in return
To live is risk dying
To hope is to risk despair
To try is to risk failure

But risk must be taken, because the
greatest hazard in life is to risk nothing
The person who risks nothing, does
nothing has nothing and is nothing
They may avoid suffering and sorrow
But they cannot learn, feel, change, grow
love or live

Chained by their certitude, they are a
slave, they forfeited.
They have forfeited their freedom
Only a person that risks
Is truly free

If There's Light in the Soul

If there's light in the soul
There'll be beauty in the person
If there's beauty in the person
There'll be harmony in the house
If there's harmony in the house
There'll be order in the nation
If there's order in the nation
There'll be peace in the world.

My Darkness

My darkness was like a long tunnel
with no end
With a glimmer of light at the top.
But seem I was never able to reach the top
and go into the light.
Always sliding down to the bottom
Then one day I finally climbed out of
the darkness
Now my life is full of colours
No more darkness

We aspire to the top to look for rest
It lies at the bottom
Water rest only when it gets to the
lowest place
So do men
Hence be lowly

Things can never go badly wrong
If the heart be true and the love be strong;
For the mist, if it comes,
And the weeping rain
Will be changed by the
Love into sunshine again

So as up hill we all journey,
Let us scatter all the way,
Kindly words, for they are sunshine
In the dark and cloudy day.

Do not grudge no loving word or action,
As a long through life we go!
There are weary ones around you;
If you love them—tell them so

It is not always those who breathe,
Who live;
It is not always those who have
Who give
But there are lives whose live
Work is so done
That one brief life is so many
Lives in one

<u>Wife</u>

What is there in the vale of life
Half so, delightful as a wife,
When friendship, love and peace combine
To stamp the marriage divine.

<u>What if</u>

I thought to do a kindly deed,
But time slipped by too fast;
The deed is still undone—ah me
My chance forever past.
I meant to speak a cheery word:
Before what word was said,
This idle word distracted me,
And now my friend id dead.

<u>Be Open</u>

Why is dew on one flower and not on a
other, because one opens its cup and
takes it in
While the other chooses itself and the
drops run off.
God rains his goodness and mercy as
widespread as the dew, and if we lack
them it is because we will not open our
hearts to receive them.

<u>Beware</u>

Beware of the desperate steps,
The darkest day,
Live till tomorrow, will have passed away.

Dark Tunnel

I live in a dark tunnel seems no way out
In my dark tunnel carry my burden of
tears and fears
I climb to the top of the tunnel
many times
But never reaching the light, all slipping
to the bottom
Then I found out that the dark tunnel
is live
That I have had help to carry me so that I
do not fall by the wayside
And that the light I have been clinging to
at the top is god, light
And that by forgiving, and not hurting
people on my way
I am now able to reach the top and climb
out of my dark tunnel into the light of
beautiful rainbow colours of light.

The further one travels, the less one knows

Dawn

Dear master, what can I do to-day?
For patient and still.
I await thy will,
O speak and give me grace to obey.

There are souls that are living in
sorrow's night
Let me say a word
That may comfort afford
Or make me a quiet, shining light

I as not some grand opportunity
But love brings a sigh
Less this day should pass by
And nothing be done to glorify thee.

True love—is best of all
True love—won't let you fall
True love—will hear your call
True love—is the light of the world.

One asks why does the sun rise?
Why do birds sing
I have questioned these things
But then I found true love

I found true love
When I was deep down
In my soul sorrow
Beneath the darkest skies

He gives love to the loveless
Hope to the dispossessed
Faith to the lonely ones
Garage to the meek
True love to all.

All is not attractive that is good
Iron does not sparkle like a diamond
Yet it is useful
Gold has not the fragrance of a flower, yet
it is valuable
So different persons have different graces
of excellence, and to be just have a eye
for all

— — — — — — — — — — — — — — — — — — —

Jesus be near at either hand
Jesus behind, before me stand
Jesus with me where'er I go
Jesus around above, below

Jesus be in my heart and mind
Jesus within my soul enshrined
Jesus control my way ward heart
Jesus abide and ne'er depart

Jesus my life and only way
Jesus my lantern by night and day
Jesus be my unchanging friend
Jesus be my guide and shepherd to
the end.

The horizontal and the vertical

The horizontal—a reminder

That like Jesus I am on a pilgrim journey
That like Jesus I cannot always choose
the way
That like Jesus I carry with me a burden I
cannot lose

The vertical—a reminder

That Jesus is always there
That all I do is in thee to give him glory
That my journey to heaven must be
rooted into the ground

Peace

Deep peace of the running wave to you
Deep peace of the flowing air to you
Deep peace of the quiet earth to you
Deep peace of the shining stars to you
Deep peace of the son of peace to you.

To be open

This hard to do . . . .
I have been taught to protect myself with
my privacy
My shyness
My self-imposed loneliness
My property

If only I can take the risk
To be open to others . . . .
To be patient with them . . . .
To waste time with them
Than I shall learn to believe in them and
they to believe in me.

This takes time . . . more even than three
Months . . . and love . . . but the reward is
Jesus himself . . . for Jesus is love

God's spirit falls on me as dewdrops
on a rose

If I but like a rose my heart to
him enclose,

In all eternity no tone can be so sweet

As where man's heart with god unison
doth beat.

<u>Do the Right</u>

Perish policy and cunning
Perish all that fears the light

Whether losing, whether winning
Trust in god and do the right
Some will hate thee
Some will love thee
Cease from man and look above thee
Trust in god and do the right

If there's a song that I can sing
Or a word that I can say

To cheer the world, or comfort the world,
Let me utter them while I may,
For who, shall be soothed by the
silent note,
Of the song that remains unsung
Or gather joy from the voiceless words
That sleep in a deadmans tongue?

Safety

He that is down
Need fear no fall
He that is low
No pride
He that is humble ever shall
Have god to be his guide.

Don't lay up trouble
Nor let a thought

Of sweet revenge possess you
When tales untruthful
Reach your ears

That trouble and distress you

Now chase the wrong with bated breath

As, lie will run itself to death.

A kindly wish to you all

I will not wish thee riches nor the glare
of greatness.

But that where'er you may go
Some weary Face may brighten at
your smile
Some weary heart may know
Sunshine for awhile

And so your years through life
Shall be a crack of light.

Like angels, footsteps passing through
the night

This life is not all roses
Maybe tis full of care
But I do have roses in my heart
And birds sing ever there.

Our Unseen Guide

I do not try to see my way,
Before, behind, or right

I cannot tell what dangers hurt
Or do haunt my steps, nor even
At what height I may be
Above sea my path does wind
For I am blind

Yet its not without a guide I do wind
My unseen way, by day
By night

Close by my side there walks a friend
Strong, tender, true
I trust his sight

He sees my way before, behind
Though I am blind.

Poverty

Our lord never mentions poverty as
One of the obstructions to his kingdom
Neither has it ever proved such
Riches, cares and desires he does mention

Time is god's loan and character
His interest

What is there in this life
Half so delightful as a wife
When friendship, love and peace combine
To stamp the marriage bond divine

The Pen

They say the pen is mighty than
Sword, I believe its true

The pen can bring war and peace too
For it was the pen that broth
Peace in our time, said was the pen
That we never it so good
But some said they had.

For it's the pen that broth us good news,
telling it was for the good and the true.

For it was the pen that wrote the bible
That brought me to new life too

There is dew on one flower and not on
another, because one is open takes it in

While the other closes itself, and the
drops run off.

God rains his goodness and mercy
As widespread as the dew, and if we
Lack him. It is because we will not open
our hearts to receive them

<u>Now</u>

I thought to do a kindly deed
But time slipped by too fast

The deed is still undone—ah, me
My chance for ever past

I meant to speak a cheery ward
Before that word was said

The idle world distracted me
And now my friend is dead!!

I want to give others hope and faith
I want to do all that the master said
I want to live right from day to day
I'm sure I shall not pass again this way

The bread that bringeth strength I
want to give

The water pure that bids thirsty live

I want to help the life fainting day by day
I'm sure I shall not pass again this way

If we had but a Day

We should fill the hours with the
sweetest things
if we had but a day
we should drink alone at the
purest springs
In our upward way
We should love with a lifetimes
Love in a hour
If the hours were few
We should rest, not for dreams
But for fresher power
To be and to do
We should waste no moments in
weak regret
If the day were one
If we remember and what we forget
Went out with the sun
We should be from our glamorous
Selves set free

To work or to pray
And to be what the father would
Have us be
If we had but a day

Nothing is lost

To talk with god—no breath is lost
Talk on talk on

To walk with god—no strength is lost
Walk on walk on

To wait on god—no time is lost
Wait on wait on

To work the axe—no work is lost
Work on work on

The work is quicker, better done

Not needing half the strength laid on
Work on work on

If you put a little loving into all the work
you do
And a little bit of gladness and a
Little be of you
And a little bit of sweetness and a little bit
of a song
Not a day will seen to toils one
Not a day will seen to long

BOOK 2

The Mind Ripple

A man sitting by a lake he was throwing small pebbles into it from time to time.
A young boy happened to cross by.
He was intrigued to see that after every few minutes or so, the man would toss a pebble into the lake.
The boy went up to the man and said, good pastime, this stone throwing, he?
"Hmmm, said the man, he seemed to be deep in thought and obviously did not wish to be disturbed.
Sometime later the man said softly, look at the water, it is absolutely still.
The boy said "yeah it is"
The man tossed a pebble into the water and continued, only till I toss a pebble into it now you see the ripples?
Yeah said the boy they spread further and further, and soon the water is still again offered the man.

The boy said sure, it becomes quiet after
a while.

The man continued, what if we want to stop
the ripples, the root cause of the ripples is the
stone. Lets take the stone out. Go ahead and
look for it, the boy put his hand into the water
and tried to take the stone out.

But he only succeeded in making more ripples.

He was able to take the stone out, but the
number of ripples that were made in the process
were a lot more than before.

The wise man said "it is not possible to stop the
movement of the water once a pebble has been
thrown into it.

But if we can stop ourselves from throwing
the pebble in the first place, the ripples can be
avoided altogether.

So too, it is with our minds.

If a thought enters into it, it creates ripples.

The only way to save the mind from getting
disturbed is to block and ban the entry of every
superfluous thought that could be potential
cause for disturbance.

If a disturbance has entered into the mind, it
will take its own time to die down.

Too many conflicting thoughts just cause more
and more disturbance.
Once the disturbance has been caused it takes
time to ebb out.
Even trying forcibly to remove the thought may
further increase the turmoil in the mind.
Time surely is a great healer but prevention is
always better than cure.
Before you allow a thought or a piece of
information to enter your mind, put it through
the triple filter test of authenticity, goodness
and value.

Lost Mind

Saturday I lost my keys to my home,
Then when I went to pay in the shop could not
find my wallet.
As I did that I remember I had just put it in a
different pocket,
I had only lost my mind.

We want a peaceful life

We often say that we want a peaceful life
We wish to be at a place where there is no noise,
No trouble or no hard work.
But this does not actually mean peace.
To be in the midst of chaos of life
And still be calm in your heart.
. . . . is what "peace" is

Life's Mystery

I don't know why we are here
It's a mystery to us all
We had no choice in the first place
It's a place thy sent us all

They say its god's creation the mountains,
land, sea, the moon, stars, the earth, the cold
the rain, the sun, the wind that blows.

All kinds of animals are here to see
The birds, the bees, the flowers, the trees,
The air that we breathe.

Now its time for meditation,
To give more thought to recreation,
Myths and legends,
Tales of yore, only help to baffle us more

If I could see a reason why,
As I gaze along the big wide sky

I wonder who could build a roof so tall
What is the purpose of it all?

If as I gaze at the infinity of the sky
So great a vault, so wide and tall,
I wonder if I may, before I die
Grasp something of the purpose of it all.

Who am I

Who am I, I often ask myself this question.
Who am I the child who was always running,
hiding away scared and frightened of adults.
Or am I the adult who for four years had peace
in his mind, who was not frightened of anyone.

Am I the person now, who keeps returning to my
childhood, still running scared and frightened,
And hurting myself, full of depression and
anxiety, looking over all these people not
recognising who I am
Wishing I was the adult in the middle full of
peace again.

I am always feeling that I am not good enough
at anything I do
I lead my life as if I am in a dark mine
Looking for the light!
People have said
Even in the darkest mine
A diamond does shine out.

Pens and War's, Peace

Thy say the pen is mighty than the sword,
I believe it to be true for it was the pen that
brought peace in our time.
It also brings news of friends passing and joy of
new arrivals, and the good news for all.

<u>Darkness</u>

I live my life in darkness, always looking for
colour in it,
I know the darkness is my past and fear of not
coping; colour is freedom and peace of mind,
I will find it one day again
O to live in life's colour

Risks

To laugh is to risk appearing the fool
To weep is to risk appearing sentimental
To reach out is to risk involvement
To expose feelings is to risk exposing your true self
To place ideas, your dreams before a crowd is to
risk their loss
To love is to risk not being loved in return
To live is to risk dying
To hope is to risk despair
To try is to risk failure

But risks must be taken because the greatest
hazard in life is to risk nothing
The person who risks nothing, does nothing,
has nothing and is nothing
They may avoid suffering and sorrow, but they
cannot learn, feel, change, grow, love or live
Chained by their certitude, they are a slave, they
have forfeited their freedom
Only a person that risks is free.

Bogeyman

Do you remember the days,
When you used to run to school
Always avoiding the grates
On the path or in the road,
Why, you might ask!
Because of !!Bogeyman!!

Bogeyman lived in the dark,
In the coal cellars drives.
Where they waited to catch little boys
Yes I remember well those days
I still don't walk over grates,
On paths or roads
He, still waiting!!

I SAW SOME LOVELY THINGS TODAY

I saw some lovely things today:
I feel, dear god, I'd like to pray.
I saw some tiny, little things –
Some hummingbirds with gauzy wings,
A flower with its head held high
As though it's blue came from the sky.
I saw some lovely things today:
I feel, dear god, I'd like to pray.

I heard some wondrous things today:
I feel, dear god, I'd like to pray.
I heard a brook. It seemed to me
To catch the rhythm of the sea.
I heard a bird, it sang to me
A joyous, Lilting melody
I heard some wondrous things today:
I feel, dear god, I'd like to pray.

Perhaps, dear lord, the woodland air
Was really breathing out a prayer—
The prayer I prayed.
The awe and wonder in my heart
Were such a very vital part
Of what thou callest prayer.

A MORNING PRAYER

O God, Lord of all good life, help me to use
today well.
Help me to use today:
To know you a little better
To do my work a little more diligently
To serve my fellow men a little more lovingly
To make myself, with your help a little more
like Jesus.
Help me make today a day of progress in my
life, and to become a little more like you want
me to be.

This I ask for Jesus
Amen

Lightning Source UK Ltd.
Milton Keynes UK
UKOW04f0315120315

247741UK00001B/15/P